balm
of
gilead

Lilian B. Yeomans, M.D.

Gospel Publishing House/Springfield, Mo. 65802

02-0728

© 1936, 1964
Revised Edition Published 1973 by Gospel Publishing House,
Springfield, Missouri 65802-1894.

7th Printing 1993

ISBN 0-88243-728-3

Printed in the United States of America

Contents

Foreword

Long ago, a lonely hill,
 Crosses three, I see them still!
Long ago the Saviour said,
 As He bowed His dying head,
  "It is finished."

Balm of Gilead, Heal my wound,
 Make me whole and strong and sound,
Thou the Medicine I take,
 Forth with speed my health doth break,
  "It is finished."

"Is there no balm in Gilead: is there no physician there?" (Jeremiah 8:22). That there is balm in Gilead and a Physician there is clearly implied, for the prophet goes on to inquire, "Why then is not the health of the daughter of my people recovered?" In the 46th chapter, verse 11, of the same prophecy the daughter of Egypt is exhorted to go up to Gilead and take balm, and is assured that it is vain for her to take "many medicines," as she will not be cured in that way.

In Ezekiel 27:17, we find that Judah traded in wheat, honey, oil, and balm. There we have the gos-

pel: wheat — life; honey — the sweetness of the Bride-
groom's love of the coming One; oil — the fullness of
the Holy Spirit; and balm — healing. Balm of Gilead!
What does Gilead mean? Perpetual Fountain.
"The water that I shall give him shall be in him a well
of water springing up into everlasting life" (John 4:
14). There is no limit of the Balm of Gilead, the healing of the Perpetual Fountain, for we are told in
Revelation 22:17, "Whosoever will, let him take the
water of life *freely*."

Why then is not the health of the daughter of
God's people recovered? Because they have "forsaken
the fountain of living waters and hewed them out
cisterns, broken cisterns, which will hold no water"
(Jeremiah 2:13).

But if we have forgotten or ignored the Physician
of Gilead, He has not forsaken us and His sweet voice
"like bells at evening pealing" still calls over land
and sea, "Come unto me all ye . . . heavy laden, and
I will give you rest."

This little book is a faint echo of His gracious invitation.

Lilian B. Yeomans, M.D.

Introduction

What are our rights as to physical healing and health? All that was purchased for us by the sacrifice of Calvary, sealed to us by the glorious resurrection of the Lord Jesus Christ, is ours by right divine.

How can we ascertain *exactly* what was secured for us? In one way only and that is a constant, careful, diligent, reverent, prayerful study of God's Word. How lacking we all are on this line!

It seems to me that God had to allow me to go down to the very gates of death and the brink of a dishonored grave to *make* me study the Word on healing.

Sometimes when I see people, ostensibly studying their Bibles on the Lord for the body, turning the leaves carelessly, looking perhaps to the right or left as someone or something attracts their attention, I cannot restrain my righteous indignation.

In mental vision I see the sick and afflicted ones writhing in physical agony and mental despair on their beds of suffering waiting for messengers of healing.

As the book of Job says, they are exceedingly scarce, "One among a thousand." Alas! How often these poor sufferers wait in vain for an "interpreter," or one who can bring them into vital contact with the Christ who died that they might have life, and have it more abundantly.

If it is our inalienable right to enjoy health through the work accomplished on Calvary, it is our solemn responsibility to make this "saving health [known] among all nations" (Psalm 67:2). To qualify for this ministry a study of the Word of God on this subject, that makes it an integral part of our beings, is absolutely essential.

When I practiced medicine, it was customary for physicians to carry certain drugs on their persons. If you were a doctor you had at hand powerful stimulants to revive the dying, anodynes to relieve intolerable physical anguish, and other emergency remedies.

When we as messengers enter sick-rooms, we should radiate from every part of our beings the power of the living Word. To this end it is necessary to study in accordance with instructions in Proverbs 4:20-23. "My son, attend to my words; incline thine ear unto my sayings. Let them not depart from thine eyes; keep them in the midst of thine heart. For they are life unto those that find them, and health to *all their flesh.*"

What does God demand here? First, undivided attention. When God says "attend," He means *"attend."* Put every other thing out of your mind. Concentrate all your faculties on the Word of God. Second, drink it in through the eargate. Open your ears to God's sayings. Close them to all else. He demands the exclusive use of eargate. He says "incline" your ear to His sayings. You don't understand? You don't have to. But you have to bow before Him and say, "Thy word is Truth." Third, you are to look as well as listen. "Let them not depart from thine eyes." "Keep your vision fixed on Jesus." There is life, physical as well as spiritual, for a look to the Lamb of God. Fourth "Keep them." Where? In the very core of your being. David said, "Thy word have I hid in my heart that I might not sin against thee" (Psalm 119:11). What did he hide? God's Word. Where did he hide it? In his heart. For what purpose? That he might not sin against God. When sin goes, sickness has to go too. They came in together, and they have to go out together. "Ye shall serve the Lord, your God, and He shall bless thy bread, and thy water; and I will take sickness away from the midst of thee" (Exodus 23:25). Fifth, the result of this — "Life . . . and health to all your flesh." All is all; brain, eyes, ears, arteries, nerves, veins, heart, lungs, glands, stomach, spleen, liver, intestines, kidneys, muscles, bones; in short, every part of you.

If you meet God's conditions, "There shall no plague come nigh thy dwelling"; "Though a thousand fall at your side and ten thousand at your right hand it shall not come nigh thee." "Thy dwelling" means the tabernacle of clay in which you sojourn as well as the certain house on a certain street in a certain town where you receive your mail.

God can and will preserve us physically, as well as spiritually, under all conditions. Let us look at some of His gracious dealings with His ancient people, the Israelites.

The Egyptians, who comprised the greatest empire on earth at the time, sought to destroy the Israelites by hard bondage, "But the more they afflicted them, the more they multiplied and grew" (Exodus 1:12). When Pharaoh ordered the destruction of the Hebrew male children at birth, the women doctors who were the obstetricians of the day, reported that the order could not be carried out as the Hebrew women were so "lively," i.e., full of vitality and vigor that they needed no assistance and could take care of themselves and their babies too (Exodus 1:19).

When the Israelites went out of Egypt, there was not one feeble person among the tribes though Egypt was decimated with disease (Psalm 105:37).

God put a "difference" between the Egyptians and Israel (Exodus 11:7). "I will bring none of these diseases upon thee, which I have brought upon the Egyptians: for I am the Lord that healeth thee" (Exodus 15:26).

Why the difference? Because the blood of the Passover Lamb was shed, and God said, "When I see the blood, I will pass over you, and the plague shall not be upon you to destroy you, when I smite the land of Egypt" (Exodus 12:13). Thank God that the Blood is still ours, our sure defense! For we read, "They overcame him [Satan] by the blood of the Lamb, and by the word of their testimony" to its power (Revelation 12:11). So let us extol it and put to flight all the armies of the aliens!

1

"Satan Hath Desired to Have You . . . But"

Some time ago the Lord drew my attention to Luke 22:31, 32, and said, "There is your life story. Satan hath desired to have you, but I have prayed for you that your faith should not fail. Now strengthen the brethren."

And as I meditated on·these words I realized that Satan was one of the first personages with whom I became acquainted. I was but a little child when it happened.

Perhaps you inquire anxiously, "Were you brought up among heathen or godless and vicious people?" By no means. My people were members of a fashionable church with stained glass windows, a wonderful tower, and a choir of artists. They stood high in the esteem of the community. Perhaps they were too refined to mention Satan and warn me of his devices. And our clergy, with the low, deep tones and the exquisite manners, were so lovely that one would never dream they had ever heard of Satan. How did I, a child, become acquainted with such an undesirable individual? He introduced himself to me and he always said, "You are a naughty girl, and I am going to

11

get you." That was partly true and partly a lie. And a lie that is partly true is the hardest kind of lie to fight.

It was true that I was a naughty girl. The Holy Spirit convicted me of sin when I was very small. But it was not true that Satan was going to get me. He tried hard, as he did for Peter, but thank God! the One who prayed for Peter prayed for me too; and His prayer prevailed.

When the Civil War broke out, my father was a surgeon, practicing in Canada. He was a good surgeon and responded to the appeal for aid which he received. Surgeons are always in great demand in war time. He remained a surgeon in the U. S. Army till his death, and my mother received a pension from the Government.

One of my first remembrances is of entering a great hotel in Washington, D.C., with my father and mother and two tiny sisters. I was able to walk alone and headed the little procession. Mother held the baby in her arms and father led the older baby by the hand.

As I walked in, fresh from a Canadian town where there were no black people, a figure almost gigantic in stature, gorgeously attired, and with a face as black as ebony, advanced to meet me. I was dumb with horror and amazement. No doubt I was sure that it was Satan himself. I realize now that he must have been a magnificently proportioned Negro, exceedingly handsome. But to me he looked like the devil himself coming after me. Petrified into a small marble image with terror, I saw him advance and pick me up in his arms to bear me away. Then the floodgates opened wide. I yelled as perhaps no child the ebony gentleman had ever seen or heard had yelled. He hastily dropped me. He was more frightened than I was and I was nearly in convulsions. Employed at the hotel he was accustomed to carrying the tiny tots in, but he had not reckoned with a little green Canuck.

I escaped that time from the one I thought to be Satan, but the real Satan is not always so easily dismissed.

I grew older and went to Sunday school where I learned my "Duty to My Neighbor" — to love him as myself, to do unto all men as I would they should do unto me; to love, honor, and succor my father and mother; to honor and obey the civil authority; to submit myself to all my governors, teachers, spiritual pastor and masters; to order myself lowly and reverently to all my betters; to hurt nobody by word or deed; to bear no malice nor hatred in my heart; to keep my hands from picking and stealing, and my tongue from evil speaking, lying, and slandering; not to covet or desire other men's goods, but to learn and labor truly to get my own living; and to do my duty in that state of life unto which it shall please God to call me.

Perhaps you might think that all that good counsel would have helped me; but it worked the other way, for Satan said, "That's all right, but you haven't done it. I'm going to get you." So things grew worse than ever.

One day when my dear mother was dressing me for Sunday school in a white dress, with all its frills and tucks and fluffy ruffles — I had to hold my hands out horizontally for fear of mussing it — the awful thought of my black heart inside of my white dress and of Satan who was going to get me so overwhelmed me that I burst into a storm of weeping and cried, "I am lost! I am lost!" My mother was terrified at first — she was not saved then — but when she realized that it was my soul and not my body I was wailing about, she said, "I only wish you hadn't found it out when you had your best dress on."

With no one to guide me I drifted along trying to banish the thought of Satan and to have as good a time as possible under the circumstances.

Schools, college, and universities suceeded one another in rapid succession. By the time I graduated in medicine I was practically an agnostic. I became so hardened that I absolutely hated the missionaries who were at college with me. "Ye are the salt of the earth," and their Christlikeness convicted me, for I was a sinner and knew it.

Satan did not worry me so much now. He almost made me believe there was no devil. He was sure he had me.

But the Lord Jesus Christ hadn't forgotten to pray for me. Blessed Lord Jesus, who ever liveth to make intercession for us! He proved in my case able to save to the uttermost.

I finished my work in college and hospitals and went to Canada to practice in partnership with my mother, Dr. Amelia Le Sueur Yeomans. She was a very brilliant woman who was vice-president of the Canadian W.C.T.U. and president of the Suffrage Club. (I can always get a hearing in Canada, for people think I am my own mother and come to my meetings.)

I worked very hard in my profession, both in private practice and hospital work. The burden of responsibility was crushing and the strain terrible. Sometimes, when it seemed more than I could stand I resorted to narcotics. One awful day I awoke to the fact that I was an absolute slave to morphine. How I struggled for deliverance!

But Satan, my ancient enemy, taunted me and said

"There's no hope. No one ever gets delivered in the last stages, and that's where you are. You are my slave forever. I've got you! *I've got you!* I'VE GOT YOU!"

Thank God that I come from a long line of Puritan ancestors on my father's side! They were people who unhesitatingly believed every word in the Bible. They knew that there is a real live devil. I saw the old family Bible with the names of my forebears — one of them was "O Be Joyful Yeomans." I have always envied him (or her, I don't know which it was) the name. I had a Grandfather Yeomans who was a preacher and lived more in heaven than on earth. No doubt he claimed me among all his descendants.

Let me assure you that *God answers prayer!* Now in a moment of absolute despair there came to me the thought, "Unless there's hope for me in the Bible, there's no hope anywhere." So I shut myself up with the Book, "the only Book," as Sir Walter Scott called it. And there I found *the living Christ,* who had been praying for me all along, though I had not known it.

I was so sick, so weak, so almost demented, that I *couldn't* pray, but then I would breathe a sigh to Him, "Lord Jesus, I am past praying now. You must pray for me." And He did.

He made me know that I was accepted in Him, and He prayed a prayer in me that I would never have dared to utter, so fully did He identify Himself with me in all my awful failure. It was, "Thou wilt not leave my soul in hell, nor suffer thy Holy One to see corruption" (Acts 2:27).

Thank God for such a Saviour, who went down to the profoundest depths of the horrible pit in which I lay weltering and brought me up by the power of His resurrection!

2

Feeling and Healing

Before I was saved God graciously sent me many of His faithful messengers who told me of my awful condition and inevitable doom if I remained in it.

Once a most venerable old man, a stranger, addressed me on the streets of New York and told me, without any ceremony, that he did it because he could discern my need of salvation. And I was holding my head as high as anybody on the avenue! But the old man was right for all that. Oh, how hungry my heart was for God, the living God!

Then there was the old Salvation Army soldier who did my laundry and always gave me a good stiff warning and exhortation, even stiffer than the collars she did up for me. And there was Sarah! I shall never forget her. I met her in an institution; and she always sang, "On Christ, the Solid Rock I Stand," as she worked. Whether it was sweeping, washing, potato peeling, or scrubbing, it made no matter. She never left the solid Rock.

I was impressed and interested. I realized that these good people possessed something that I lacked and greatly needed. I noticed, however, that some of them did not always seem to be certain about their salvation; and I used to think, "That would never satisfy me. I must have something that doesn't depend on my feelings, for I know that they are apt to vary with circumstances."

One day I came across some writing by the late F. B. Meyer, of England, in which he gave his testimony to salvation. He said, "I am saved, and if the whole world stood against me I would say, 'Stand thou on that side, for on this am I. *I am saved.*' Nothing can make me doubt God's Word."

And I said to myself, "That's the kind of salvation I want." And I began to seek for it and I found it *in the Bible*. I saw there that I was saved because of *Calvary*. I'm not saved because I feel good, but because the Lord Jesus Christ bore my sins in His own body on the cross. "Thou shalt call his name Jesus; for *he* shall save his people from their sins" (Matthew 1:21). "When he had *by himself* purged our sins" (Hebrews 1:3). And the One who did the work "by *himself*" cried, "It is finished!" (John 19:30). Believe the Word and your feelings will fall in line with it.

Healing is part of salvation. The blood that was shed on the cross fully atoned for the whole race and provided perfect cleansing for every guilty soul. He tasted death for every man (Hebrews 2:9). The breaking of His sacred body by the atrocities that deprived Him of the semblance of humanity guaranteed "perfect soundness" to our bodies (Acts 3:16). "By his stripes ye were healed" (1 Peter 2:24).

Because He bore those stripes for your healing, there is no power in earth or hell that can place disease on you, or hold it there. You are free! But you have to believe God's Word. "He sent his word and healed them" (Psalm 107:20). The only way to take the medicine is to believe it, no matter how you feel. "Thy word is truth" (John 17:17).

When you let symptoms and feelings make you doubt that you were healed (*past tense*) by those stripes that the Lord Jesus Christ bore for you, you simply turn off the healing power, the heavenly electricity.

How do you think Job *felt* during his awful affliction? (He evidently had leprosy, at least I would judge so from his symptoms.) We know how he felt, for we have in the third chapter of the book the most eloquent expression of despair ever uttered in human language. We know that his flesh was rotting off, his breath like a graveyard, his fitful sleep tormented with awful visions; but what did he believe, nay *know?* "I know that my redeemer liveth." My Redeemer, the One who redeems me — liveth. Three diamonds strung on a chain that cannot break — I know. *Know* — what's feeling compared to knowing? Give me knowledge every time. Away with "I feel." I don't care what I feel when I know! I know that He is my Redeemer and that He liveth; and because He lives, I live and shall live forever. I live this moment. My Redeemer liveth and is doing His work. What is His work? Redeeming me. From what does He redeem me? From the curse of the broken law which includes every disease that flesh is heir to. "Christ hath redeemed us from the curse of the law, being made a curse for us" (Galatians 3:13).

What remains for us but praise?

3

Walking on Water

"And . . . Jesus constrained his disciples to get into a ship, and to go before him unto the other side, while he sent the multitudes away. And when he had sent the multitudes away, he went up into a mountain apart to pray: and when the evening was come, he was there alone. But the ship was now in the midst of the sea, tossed with waves: for the wind was contrary. And in the fourth watch of the night Jesus went unto them, walking on the sea. And when the disciples saw him walking on the sea, they were troubled, saying, It is a spirit; and they cried out for fear. But straightway Jesus spake unto them, saying, Be of good cheer; it is I; be not afraid. And Peter answered him and said, Lord, if it be thou, bid me come unto thee on the water. And he said, Come. And when Peter was come down out of the ship, he walked on the water, to go to Jesus. But when he saw the wind boisterous, he was afraid; and beginning to sink, he cried, saying, Lord, save me. And immediately Jesus stretched forth his hand, and caught him, and said unto him, O thou of little faith, wherefore didst thou doubt? And when they were come into the ship, the wind ceased. Then they that were in the ship came and worshiped him, saying, Of a truth thou art the Son of God" (Matthew 14:22-33).

Every four years the eyes of the world are turned on the Olympics where the best athletes of all nations compete for perishable crowns and fleeting honors. Paul says, "They do it to obtain a corruptible crown; but we an incorruptible" (1 Corinthians 9:25). And he urges us in connection with the heavenly race, "So run, that ye may obtain" (1 Corinthians 9:24).

As we are specially told that we are a "spectacle to angels" (1 Corinthians 4:9), I think we have a right to believe that those in that heavenly city are intensely interested in our prowess.

Part of Peter's race ran through water where there was no foothold for the natural man. Peter succeeded in walking on the water, but Peter also failed in walking on the water.

What a valuable lesson this incident has for us, for from it we can learn how to succeed in walking on the water and how not to fail in walking on the water.

First, note that this opportunity for water-walking was God-given. Many things contributed toward making the test a very hard one: the darkness of the night, the violence of the tempest, the frailty of the ship, the weirdness of the hour (between 3 and 6 a.m. when all vital forces are at their lowest ebb), and above all the absence of Jesus. And when the Lord at last came to them it was in an unfamiliar guise, a gleam through the gloom. But He spoke and they knew His voice! There is no voice like His.

It is said that the great tenor Caruso once called for a registered letter in a village where he was unknown. The clerk refused to deliver it without identification. The tenor hesitated a moment, then stepped back a little and opening his mouth poured forth a Niagara of glorious, golden melody that almost lifted the clerk out of his skin and set the people running to the post office from every direction. They knew his voice.

And Jesus said, "Be of good cheer; it is I; be not afraid." No wonder Peter wanted to go to Him, water or no water. But he was not fanatical, for he said to the Lord, "*Bid* me come unto thee on the water." There's a difference between faith and fanaticism. Faith refuses to take one step unless she has the Word of God under her feet, whereas fanaticism is ready to be guided by feelings and impressions alone. George Mueller said, "I must have the Word before I move."

The Lord Jesus said to Peter, "Come." Blessed Jesus! He always says "Come," never "Go." But there is a day coming when He will say "Depart." God grant that no reader of this may hear that awful word from His lips!

And Peter stepped out of the boat, left all human aid and *walked* on the water to go to Jesus. He walked on the water, and if he walked one foot he could have walked ten miles just as well.

Then he failed to walk and began to sink. Why? The Bible tells us exactly why. Let us study it so we will not fail to walk on water when it comes in our race.

"He saw the wind boisterous" — he had no business to see it for he should have been looking at One only, His objective — the Lord Jesus. And when he saw, he was afraid.

Many times this remarkable verse has helped me in crises. When I was addicted to morphine and at my last gasp, I had a lovely friend, a beautiful woman, cultured, wealthy, and, most important, deeply spiritual. She lived in her Bible and lived it out in her daily life. I never knew a woman of her refinement who had such tender compassion for outcast girls as she possessed. She took them into her beautiful home and gave them of her best.

She and I had a strange experience that drew us very close together. We were dying at the same time, she of a malignant growth, I of morphine addiction, hopeless cases both of them.

We used to sit together "beside the silent sea," waiting the sound of "the muffled oar" with our Bibles open in front of us. As we turned the leaves we found them "leaves of healing," for there was divine healing on every page. But we could not seem to grasp it, for there was a stretch of water to be walked upon.

How to take the leap? Yet it must be done if we were to survive. We were not afraid to go, and yet we felt as though we *ought* to be healed in view of God's promises.

At last I somehow got out of the boat and walked on the water. I think God had to make it nearly capsize to get me out. When I saw the waves boisterous and I sank, He caught me. By this time my lovely friend had been taken by her devoted husband to some sanitarium where, though I tried my best, I could not reach her. I never saw her again.

Very recently I had a deliverance through this passage. For some time, possibly as the result of doing a great deal of manual work to which I was not accustomed, I suffered from pain, at times excruciating. I became so stiff that it was all but impossible for me to move. My spine was particularly affected.

Satan, who is an expert diagnostician, gave my trouble a name, but I shall not flatter him by according him any publicity. He also gave me a prognosis painted in the most lurid colors. I prayed and got relief but failed to obtain complete victory. One morning in the very early hours, I said, "Well, I hardly feel able to get up at all. I suppose the Lord won't talk to me if I don't."

Then I heard that Voice. He said, "Walk on the water. You have been looking for improvements in symptoms, a change in the natural order of things. Stop it. That isn't it at all. My word is absolutely true. My healing is supernatural. It doesn't matter how you feel. *Step out.*" And I did.

A spiritual song the Lord gave my sister Amy has been singing in the air and in my spirit ever since.

Drear was the hour, tossed with the bark,
A spirit seemed coming to them through the dark,
Walking the waters, whoever heard?
Someone cried joyful, "See 'tis the Lord."

Refrain
Step out like Peter, walk upon the water,
Step out like Peter, walk upon the sea! Come!
Step out like Peter, walk upon the water,
Step out like Peter. Thy Lord will walk with thee.

"Lord, if it be Thou, bid me to come,
Walking beside Thee the waves are my home.
Off with my fisher's coat, now for the sea.
Seeing Thee only I walk with Thee."

Boisterous the billows, Peter looked round;
"Lord, in this tempest I'll surely be drowned.
Sinking I perish, Lord pull me out!"
Kind was the answer, "Why didst thou doubt?"

Some walk quite boldly with Christ on the land,
Joyful and eager to fill His command;
But should He call them to Him on the sea,
Fainting and fearful their poor hearts would be.

4

Happiness and Health

We are *commanded* to be joyful. "Be glad and rejoice" (Joel 2:21). Joy, even poor human joy, is the greatest stimulant, the most powerful restorative, the most effective tonic I know anything about in this world.

What is the greatest joy, the most blissful experience in the natural order that a human being can have? I am going to give you my opinion about it. You will find this joy spoken of in the Bible — everything is there. It is the joy of the mother when her firstborn comes into the world. The Bible tells us that this joy is so great that it swallows up all remembrance of anguish (John 16:21).

When I practiced medicine, my favorite tonic for my little mothers was letting them see their tiny babies, hold them in their arms, and gloat over them as often as possible. And, oh, the dose was such a sweet one! Sarah said that God had made her laugh so that all that heard her had to laugh with her when He gave her Isaac.

But there is a much more poignant joy than any that earth can give, and God wants us to have it con-

24

stantly. It is also the most effective tonic in existence, for God says, "The joy of the Lord is your strength" (Nehemiah 8:10).

We are *commanded* to be joyful, and part of the punishment for failure to obey this command is being laid open to the inroads of every kind of disease.

Could anything be plainer than the following scripture? "Because thou servedst not the Lord thy God with joyfulness, and with gladness of heart . . . therefore shalt thou serve thine enemies which the Lord shall send against thee. . . . Moreover He will bring thee all the diseases of Egypt, which thou wast afraid of; and they shall cleave unto thee. Also every sickness, and every plague, which is not written in the book of this law, them will the Lord bring upon thee, until thou be destroyed" (Deuteronomy 28:47, 48, 60, 61).

This joyfulness does not have its rise in any earthly things or circumstances. It is as far as heaven is from earth from hysterical, senseless mirth. In olden times they used to say to young folks who were giggling in the morning, "Be careful or you will cry before night," and, alas! there was only too much truth in the homely proverb.

Whence, then, is this joy which God demands of us to be derived? The answer to this question is written so plainly in the Word that the wayfaring man need not err therein. David tells us in Psalm 43:4, "God, my exceeding joy!" Just God, in all His glorious attributes, and our eternal union with Him in Christ Jesus. Surely this is enough to fill any reasonable being with joy unspeakable and full of glory. "In whom believing ye rejoice with joy unspeakable and full of glory" (1 Peter 1:8). *Believe* and you will rejoice; doubt and you will despair.

And this supernatural joy, *the joy of the Lord,* is our strength, spiritual, mental, and physical. We are forbidden in Nehemiah 8:10 to be sorrowful. If we are not joyful and happy, we cannot be physically sound and healthy.

Some people may say, "Oh, that is all for Old Testament saints." I do not agree with them; but let us turn to the New Testament, and we shall find that it opens with a proclamation of "good tidings of great joy" (Luke 2:10). The very word "gospel" means "good news," and people are happy when they receive glad tidings.

When Mary, the mother of our Lord, entered the presence of Elisabeth, John the Baptist, yet unborn, leaped within her for joy! That was scriptural, for the Lord told His disciples, "These things have I spoken unto you . . . that your joy might be full" (John 15:11).

"The kingdom of God is righteousness, and peace and joy in the Holy Ghost" (Romans 14:17). That this joy is absolutely independent of circumstances, the letter to the Philippians called "The Joyful Letter," abundantly proves. It is a "cup running over with joy."

What were Paul's circumstances? He was a prisoner in a filthy cellar under Rome, the Mamertine Prison, a damp, dirty hole. He was Nero's prisoner, and Nero is esteemed the most repulsive monster that ever wore mortal flesh. He murdered his own mother.

Over and over again in this epistle we find words as these: "I rejoice and will rejoice," "joy of faith," "fulfil ye my joy," "I joy and rejoice," "joy and rejoice with me." He winds up with "Finally, my brethren, rejoice in the Lord." And then he can't refrain from saying it again, *Rejoice in the Lord alway: and again I say, Rejoice*" (Philippians 4:4). Paul knew how to take the *joy tonic.* Let us imitate his example.

5

The Life . . . Which Is the Blood

"The life is the blood." This is scientifically accurate and would be accepted as such by any physiologist. Do not fear that I am going to try to teach you physiology. Nothing is further from my thoughts. Is it not important? Immensely. And interesting? Fascinatingly so. But we are concerned just now with weightier matters, even the God-breathed oracles of Scripture. In the light of that Word we can find divine messages in rocks and trees and in the bodies of men and animals, for the God of the Bible is the God of nature. I am studying human blood in this chapter, viewing it as a feeble shadow and representation of the blood of Jesus Christ, the Lamb of God, by which He washed us and made us kings and priests unto God.

The subject is a vast one. I cannot do more than touch upon some outstanding matters in connection with it.

A distinguished physiologist, Trevor Heaton, M.D., Oxford University, said, speaking of the human body: "At present we can only explore the outer fringes of this extraordinary organization, and as in all scientific discovery, this is all we can hope to do." This is true

of the body as a whole and also of each of its com-
ponent parts, including the blood.

First, what is the blood? As it flows from a wound
it looks like a uniformly red liquid, but turn the microscope on it, and you find a fluid — the plasma — with
solid particles floating in it, some red, some white.
These are the corpuscles. The bright scarlet color is
due to hemoglobin, the coloring pigment of the red
corpuscles.

Second, what is its function? What does it do for
the body? *Literally everything.* Everything comes to
the body through the agency of the blood. There is a
passage in Hebrews 9:7, just three words, "not without blood," referring to the precious blood of Jesus
Christ. Sometimes I feel like saying, "Nothing without Blood."

God has given us all things richly, but above the
entrance to redemptive fullness we read, "Not without
Blood."

To be more specific about human blood, the following may be mentioned among its functions:

(a) The removal of waste and carbon dioxide,
conveying the various excrementitious materials to the
proper channels of elimination. What a fitting illustra-
tion of the cleansing power of the blood of Christ!
"How much more shall the Blood of Christ . . . purge?"
(Hebrews 9:14). "The blood of Jesus Christ, His Son,
cleanseth us from all sin" (1 John 1:7).

So important is this function in the natural order
that it has been said that nine tenths of disease is
caused by failure in elimination. Well may the apostle exhort us, "Having these promises, dearly beloved,
let us cleanse ourselves from *all* filthiness of the flesh
and spirit" (2 Corinthians 7:1).

(b) The blood carries to each cell in the body

(there are millions of them) its necessary food, making a complete circuit of the body in 45 to 50 seconds. Of the blood of Christ, the Word says, "Except ye eat the flesh of the Son of man, and *drink his blood,* ye have no life in you. . . . my blood is drink indeed" (John 6:53, 55). It is summed up in the words in Luke 22:20, "This cup *is the new testament* in my blood." Everything God has promised us comes to us through the blood of Jesus Christ.

(c) The blood aids in keeping the temperature of our bodies normal. God wants our spiritual temperature kept normal. "Because iniquity shall abound, the love of many shall wax cold" (Matthew 24:12). "Because thou art lukewarm, . . . I will spue thee out of my mouth" (Revelation 3:15). When Peter followed afar off he had to warm himself. We are brought "nigh by the blood of Christ" (Ephesians 2:13).

(d) It brings each cell of the body into contact with the atmosphere and its life-giving oxygen by means of the hemoglobin of the red blood corpuscles. The oxygen brought to the cells sets fire to the waste matter, and the ashes are carried off by the blood. In cases of hemorrhage that cannot be arrested, the patient endures unspeakable agony as every cell in the body suffers from air hunger. Never shall I forget some cases of the kind that I have witnessed, nor some cases of God-hunger I have seen. What is the remedy in hemorrhage from the blood vessels? Transfusion of blood. When we are hungry for God and cannot find Him, what do we need? The blood of Jesus, which gives us access to His presence (Hebrews 10:19).

(e) The blood also conveys emergency supplies (hormones — substances manufactured by certain organs for crises) from the place of manufacture to the organs that have to meet the emergency. For instance adrenalin, made in the little cocked-hat shaped glands (suprarenal capsules) situated on top of the kidneys, a most powerful stimulant, which is said to put the pounce into the lion; and pituatrin, the strongest restorative known, which is made by the pituitary body, a hazelnut shaped gland on the floor of the skull under the brain, are conveyed by the blood in this way. Adrenalin sometimes seems, if we can believe reports, to conquer death, for the time being. Of the blood of the Lord Jesus Christ we read that by His death on the cross He destroyed him that had the power of death, that is, the devil (Hebrews 2:14), so that saints of God can now overcome Satan by the blood of the Lamb (Revelation 12:11).

(f) Human blood defends the body by actually conquering deadly microbes when they get into the circulation. The soldiers of the blood, tiny white corpuscles, called leucocytes, stand up and fight them to the death. So the blood of the Lamb overcomes all Satan's power of sin, sickness, and death if we will but believe and use it. We are made "priests unto God" (Revelation 1:6). As priests it is our prerogative to use the *Blood*. It will bring victory every time if we do it in faith, for faith will never let go till Satan is beaten down under our feet.

(g) By its marvelous power of coagulation the blood stops bleeding, seals up the wound, and starts repair work at the point of injury. So the blood of Jesus heals our wounds, makes us "whole, and strong and sound" with "perfect soundness" (Acts 3:16).

(h) The blood continually bathes every cell in the body in tissue lymph. This is their proper atmosphere without which they could not live. The blood of Jesus Christ brings us into communion and fellow-

ship with God, the Father and His Son Jesus Christ
(1 John 1:3). God said, "I will appear in the cloud
upon the mercy seat" (the place where the blood was
sprinkled) (Leviticus 16:2). "I will commune with
thee from above the mercy seat" (Exodus 25:22).

As we study human blood we realize the truth of
the words in Romans 1:19, 20, "That which may be
known of God is manifest in them; for God hath
shewed it unto them. For the invisible things of him
from the creation of the world are clearly seen, being
understood by the things that are made, even his
eternal power and Godhead."

These things that human blood does for us are faint
pictures, shadowy representations of what the blood
of the God-Man, Christ Jesus, does for those who have
believed on Him and have life through His Name.

6

Salt

⌐The Lord Jesus Christ compares His people to salt. How apt the comparison! How true the similitude! "Ye are the salt of the earth" (Matthew 5:13).

What is salt? How is it brought into existence? By the union of two substances: one, something from above, a gas or vapor, chlorine (ancient chemists called gasses "spirits"), and second, something from below, of the earth, a dark, dull, grayish black metal, called sodium. From this union a totally new substance, sodium chloride, or salt, is born.

Of course salt is found in nature widely distributed, but all the salt so found in mines, the ocean, vegetables, etc., is formed by the union of something from above with something from beneath and is properly called, in chemical parlance, sodium chloride.

Please note that the new substance is utterly different from the dull, dark metal of the earth, sodium. It is white, pure, beautiful (in its crystalline form), healing, health-preserving, decay-preventing, characteristically different from everything else in the universe. It is salt! Nothing else will take its place.

The dark, dull, unlovely metal of the earth, represents man in his natural state — "The first man is of the earth, earthy" (1 Corinthians 15:47). In John 3:3 it says, "Except a man be born again [marginal reading 'from above'], he cannot see the kingdom of God."

Something spiritual, something from above, even the Spirit of God unites with this being of earth, and a mighty *re-creation* is effected. He is born of the Spirit, born again, born from above and becomes a new substance, or creation, in Christ Jesus. As it is utterly impossible to obtain natural salt except by the union of something from above with something from beneath, so is spiritual salt unobtainable except by the moving of the Spirit of God on the human heart.

It does not come by effort, good resolutions, or reformation; but by the Spirit of God coming upon us, the power of the Highest overshadowing us. We are born of God, made partakers of the divine nature, heirs of God, joint heirs with Christ. "Beloved, now are we the sons of God" (1 John 3:2). "Now." When? After we have believed on the Lord Jesus Christ — "Ye are the children of God by faith in Jesus Christ" (Galatians 3:26). And as salt is not sodium, so you are not the old Adam but a new creation in Christ Jesus. "Not I but Christ." White? Yes, *white* through the blood of the Lamb.

A poor girl who had been saved from awful vileness by faith in the Sacrifice of Calvary was ordered by the surgeons in the hospital where she had been placed to have an operation. She was told that ether would have to be administered. She turned pale and asked the nurse to come to her bed.

"What is the matter, dear?" inquired the nurse. "Are you afraid of the operation?"

"No, nurse, I am not afraid of that. If I should die, I have a home waiting for me in heaven. But, oh, I am so afraid that when I am intoxicated by the ether I may say something to dishonor my Lord. You don't know what awful things I have heard and said too. Will you promise me to tell me truly what I say when I come out of the anaesthetic?"

When she regained consciousness she asked the nurse if she had been quiet under the ether.

"No," said the nurse, "you were not quiet all the time."

"Oh, what did I say?"

"You did not speak but you sang."

"What did I sing?"

"Just one hymn, 'Safe in the Arms of Jesus.'"

A little girl who was dug out of a foul den and saved at a Sunday school in the slums got sick and lay dying. She sent her only penny to the Sunday school and said, "Grandmother, see that Jesus gets it all."

"Pure?" Yes; "though your sins be as scarlet they shall be as white as snow" (Isaiah 1:18).

I was much touched at the inscription on a monument erected in a New York cemetery by a number of girls of the streets who were saved in connection with a work in which I was interested. They desired to lie around it rather than anywhere else. Alas! Their lives were curtailed by their awful experiences and they themselves prepared this resting place for their bodies and chose the inscription, "These are they which came out of great tribulation, and have washed their robes, and made them white in the blood of the Lamb. Therefore are they before the throne of God" (Revelation 7:14, 15).

Beautiful? Yes, and like salt, the beauty, which is of the Lord, our God, is more apparent the closer you look at it. Viewed through a microscope salt assumes beautiful crystalline forms.

Healing, health preserving, antiseptic, causing unsound places to heal up? Yes, it is all of these, and sometimes it makes people who have these unsound places on them smart in the process of healing them.

Arresting decay, destruction, and putrefactive processes? Yes, God's salt does all of these things, for we are told to have "no fellowship with the unfruitful works of darkness, but rather reprove them" (Ephesians 5:11).

The Lord Jesus says He sends us out as the Father sent Him, and the works that He did we are to do also, and greater works. God's plan for His salt is that it should be distributed as widely as its type in the mineral world. How widely salt is distributed in the great oceans touching every shore, in the earth in combination with various minerals, in caves hung with innumerable stalactites, in vegetables and animals; in short, everywhere. So God's salt is found everywhere from hovel to palace, and He commands us to scatter it to every land till all have heard the message of salvation.

God alone knows the power that dwells in the presence of His people! For the sake of ten righteous men God was willing to avert the awful doom that fell on Sodom and Gomorrah. On Paul's eventful journey to Rome God gave him the lives of all who sailed with him, some 275 souls.

But if the salt has lost its savor, what is it good for? Nothing. A young university student who had been trained by a fine Christian mother, said to me once: "You know we have a theological faculty at the university, but I find that the students in theology don't believe the Bible. I can't help believing it, and when they don't I can't imagine why they are studying theology. What good can they be to God or man?"

The Lord answers that question — "If the salt have lost his savour, . . . it is . . . good for nothing . . . but to be cast out" (Matthew 5:13).

7

"Himself"

"Himself took our infirmities, and bare our sicknesses" (Matthew 8:17). I wish that all who read this chapter would precede it by reading Matthew 8:1-17 at least three times. Indeed, it would be well to commit the verses to memory. They seem to cast a flood of divine illumination on the whole subject of divine healing.

We must never forget that it is the Word that heals. "He sent His *word* and healed them" (Psalm 107:20). Perhaps you ask, "Does not the *word* mean the Lord Jesus Christ?" Certainly, but as we read the written Word in faith, the Lord Jesus Himself meets us in its pages.

In order to experience the full power of the Bible in healing our bodies, it is essential to have it hidden in our hearts (Proverbs 4:20). Then we can "meditate in it" day and night, let it flow through our beings, "a pure river of water of *life*, clear as crystal, proceeding out of the throne of God and of the Lamb" (Revelation 22:1).

I sometimes suggest lists of Scripture verses bearing particularly on the truth of the Lord for the body, but experience has taught me that it is much more effective for each person to make his or her own list, as they are lighted up to them by the Holy Spirit. Jot down the references and commit them to memory so that they become a part of your consciousness. In that way they are easily accessible at all times, day or night, on the street, traveling, and even when you are unwillingly compelled to listen to unprofitable conversation or radio broadcasting. By means of the memorized verses you can mount up on wings like an eagle.

Glancing at the verses in the 8th of Matthew which precede our text, "Himself" (Matthew 8:17), we have the case of the leper, who doubted the willingness of the Lord to heal while he was fully convinced of His ability to do so. Possibly the wretched creature was so conscious of his repulsiveness and the vile nature of his malady that he could not believe anyone would have mercy on such an outcast from human society. But the Lord Jesus settled that misgiving forever, for *all lepers,* no matter how loathsome, by His "*I will.*" Praise God for that!

Next a very different figure appears upon the stage. A Roman centurion (Matthew 8:5-13) enters, with dignified bearing and martial mien. The Romans were masters of the world, and they let the world know it. But how is this? His proud head is bowed before the gentle Nazarene, whom he addresses as "Lord" (Gr. *kurios*). He says, in effect, "I know what power is. Caesar has power over me, power of life and death; I have power over my subordinates, but in Thee I acknowledge power *over all power.* Speak but the word. 'Tis all I ask. I crave it as a bounty, for I am not worthy."

And then the Lord Jesus declared that He had not

found such faith in Israel, and gives him admission to the Heavenly feast where he is told his place card will be beside Abraham, Isaac, and Jacob. "And his servant was healed in the selfsame hour."

In verses 14 and 15, we have a picture of the Lord Jesus as the family Physician. I always felt the relationship of a truly good and devoted physician to the families of which he was in charge was a very sacred one. My ideal family physician, I may as well own, was my own mother. I knew how she loved her charges and truly bore them on her heart day and night. She had families, every junior member of which she had brought into the world. How they reciprocated her affection!

On one occasion she left town on a speaking tour and placed her practice in the hands of a very able doctor whose only fault was that he was a man.

One morning the children were told that the doctor was coming. This was always the cause of great rejoicing. Glad expectancy reigned among the youngsters. At last the door opened and the nurse came in and introduced a very fine looking gentleman with a bright smile on his face. But it didn't help him with the children. They had never had any doctor but Mother, and the youngest cried indignantly, "Go away! I won't have you. You aren't a doctor at all. You are a *man!*"

But how beautiful is the ministry of the Lord Jesus as the family Physician! How the children love Him! How readily the little things trust Him! They put us to shame with their simple faith. The dear old hymn, "God Will Take Care of You" was inspired by a tiny child whose mother was ill and whose father (a minister of the gospel) hesitated to leave her to fulfill his engagements. The little fellow crept up close to his mother and whispered in her ear, "Mother, God will take care of you." This so rebuked their unbelief that the father made full proof of his ministry and returned to find the mother healed and rejoicing in the beautiful song the Lord had given her. He then sat down and played the words to a tune God gave him, and so we have it:

> God will take care of you,
> Through every day, o'er all the way.
> God will take care of you.

In the 16th and 17th verses of Matthew 8 we have a mass meeting for healing, though the doctors of divinity, or at least some of them, say we have no Bible authority for holding them. "They brought unto him many that were possessed with devils: and he cast out the spirits with his word, and healed all that were sick: that it might be fulfilled which was spoken by Esaias the prophet, saying, Himself took our infirmities, and bare our sicknesses."

This mass meeting is linked by the Holy Spirit to the prophecy of Isaiah in the Atonement chapter (Isaiah 53), announcing the Messiah as the bearer of sickness and infirmity. It was not some exceptional manifestation of His power with which to convince people of His deity, but it was to fulfill His messiahship. He had to heal all who came to Him for healing, otherwise He would not have been true to the picture painted of Him by the Holy Spirit 700 years before. We can find no warrant for accepting a Christ who does not heal the sick. There is no such Christ in the Bible. We read of our Lord in 1 Corinthians 15:3 that He "died for our sins *according to the scriptures.*" The Scriptures tell us that He bore our sicknesses, as well as our sins, on that cross of shame where He died His sacrificial death. "Surely he hath borne our griefs, and carried our sorrows" (Isaiah 53:4).

"The words in Isaiah 53:4, for 'griefs,' *kholee*, and 'sorrows,' *makob*, literally mean 'sicknesses' and 'pains.'" — *Bodily Healing in the Atonement*, T. J. McCrossan.

And now the climax. It was He *Himself* who took our infirmities and bore our sicknesses. Not Himself and physicians; not Himself and surgeons. When it tells us in Hebrews 1:3 that "He, . . . by himself purged our sins," we should not dare to add one iota of human effort or merit to that supreme sacrifice. There is nothing that can be added. When the Bible tells us that He Himself forever consummated and finished our healing, can any addition be made thereto?

Dr. A. B. Simpson relates that on one occasion he had to speak on divine healing before a large audience, presumably including a large number of unsympathetic persons. He had no opportunity to make any preparation, and so asked God to mightily illuminate him by the Holy Spirit, giving him Scripture verse, subject, and sermon. One word, "Himself," was flashed into his spirit; and it was all-sufficient, for Himself is our medicine, and He never fails. He is the healing and the health. The healing cannot be had apart from Him. He is the life of our mortal bodies as well as of our spirits. It is all wrapped up in Him, and we have to receive Him in all His fullness to get the healing in its perfection. He abides in us by the Holy Spirit, and one thought of discouragement will shut out the fullness of His abiding.

He Himself took and bore, not once but for always. He is always lifting us and bearing us.

8

"How Shall I Curse Whom God Hath Not Cursed?"

The startling question of this chapter is asked by one of the most awful and mysterious personages in Holy Writ, Balaam, the son of Beor, brought from Aram, out of the mountains of the East, by Balak, king of Moab, to curse Jacob and defy Israel.

That Balaam was possessed of extraordinary powers is evident from the absolute confidence placed in him by his fellow men as represented by Balak, who said to him: "I wot that he whom thou blessest is blessed, and he whom thou cursest is cursed" (Numbers 22:6).

The wonderful testimony to God's faithfulness which he uttered, "God is not a man that He should lie; neither the son of man, that He should repent" (Numbers 23:19), and the sublime prophecy of the Messiah as the Star and Scepter that issued from his lips when for the third time Satan vainly tried to use his tool to the destruction of Israel, mark him as one singularly gifted of God.

What a tragedy that such splendid powers should have been prostituted to earn the "wages of unrighteousness"! But it is with his confession of absolute inability to accomplish that for which, with great care and effort, he was brought from the mountains of the East to do, that we are concerned.

Three times he tried; no expense was spared; money was poured out like water. No effort was too great. To the high places of Baal, seats of Satan, they betook themselves. Seven altars smoked with sacrifices of bullocks and rams. Balak and the princes of Moab with him stood by the burnt offering. Expectantly the king and his train waited for the awful word that should curse the people of God. At last the seer, prostrated by the prophetic impulse, with wide open eyes, staring yet blind to things of earth, speaks in solemn accents:

"Hath he [God] said, and shall he not do it? Or hath he spoken, and shall he not make it good? Behold I have received commandment to bless: and he hath blessed; and I cannot reverse it. He hath not beheld iniquity in Jacob, neither hath he seen perverseness in Israel; the Lord his God is with him, and the shout of a king is among them. . . . Surely there is no enchantment against Jacob, neither is there any divination against Israel" (Numbers 23:19-21, 23).

In despair Balak implores — "Neither curse them at all, nor bless them at all." But his plea is in vain. Balaam says, "If Balak would give me his house full of silver and gold, I cannot go beyond the commandment of the Lord, to do either good or bad of mine own mind; but what the Lord saith, that will I speak" (24:13).

Then from his controlled lips pour sublimely glorious prophecies of the coming Messianic kingdom: "There shall come a Star out of Jacob, and a Sceptre shall rise out of Israel. . . . Out of Jacob shall come He that shall have dominion" (24:17, 19).

Note that in every instance increased effort to curse only results in augmented blessing. Had there been iniquity in Israel? Alas the Bible makes it clear that they had repeatedly failed God. Did God condone it? Never. He condemned and punished them, but when Satan rose against them to curse them by means of his tool Balaam, He stood like a lion and defended His people. For the Rock had been smitten and abundant life-giving water (type of salvation by grace) had reached the need of the people.

The brazen serpent, type of the cross of Christ, had been lifted up in their midst and they had received life for a look. "Who shall lay anything to the charge of God's elect? It is God that justifieth" (Romans 8:33).

We read that these things "happened to them for ensamples: and are written for our admonition, upon whom the ends of the world are come." The curse for disobedience to God's commands includes every disease to which humanity is liable. This is explicitly stated in Deuteronomy 28:58-62. Satan comes with all his power and exhausts his resources to curse us with some blighting, blasting, devouring disease; but if we will look in simple faith to the One who was made a curse in our stead the enemy is inevitably defeated.

He *cannot* curse whom God has not cursed; nay more, his very efforts to do this only result in increased blessing for us. On his own confession we learn this, "Behold I have received commandment to bless: and he hath blessed; and I cannot reverse it" (Numbers 23:20).

If you are threatened with alarming symptoms in your body, *have no fear!* The children of Israel were abiding in their tents, "according to their tribes," when God wrought this mighty deliverance for them. See to it that you are in the circle of His arms, in the center of His will. If the Holy Spirit shows you that you have strayed, come home to *your tent* by the appointed path of repentance toward God and faith in the Lord Jesus Christ. Then rest securely in the knowledge that Satan *cannot* put disease (part of the curse) upon you.

Does someone ask, "But Dr. Yeomans, what about Sister So and So, or Brother This or That, who is suffering at this moment from an awful ailment, and how can you explain the case of a saint who died of a deadly disease?"

There is an answer to every legitimate question in the Bible, a solution to every problem, and I find it in this case in Deuteronomy 29:29: "The secret things belong unto the Lord our God: but those things which are revealed belong unto us and to our children forever, that we may do all the words of this law."

It is clearly *revealed* that Christ hath redeemed us from the curse of the law, including every sickness to which humanity is liable. This truth belongs to us, and our children, and we are responsible before God for the use which we make of it. Things which God has not seen fit to reveal to us at this time *are not our property,* and we do well to remember this and refrain from touching them even in thought.

The fact that the prophet Elisha, who raised the dead in his ministry, fell sick "of his sickness whereof he died" does not exonerate us from our responsibility in regard to God's provision for our healing and health; neither does it justify us in judging the prophet. If we feel any inclination to do this, it would be well for us to note that when a dead man was put into Elisha's tomb he was revived and rose to his feet the moment he touched Elisha's bones. Just so, we are healed the moment our faith *really touches* the sacrificial death of our Lord Jesus Christ on Calvary.

When I was on the very brink of the grave, the holiest person I ever met nearly rolled me in by the fact that she was so ailing and frail. The enemy would ask, "How can *you* hope to be healed when Mrs. So and So always has one foot in the grave and the other on the brink? You know you are not holy like she is and have no hope of ever being her equal spiritually. Explain her condition before you expect restoration to health."

How much precious time I wasted trying to explain Mrs. So and So's case. But one day I got desperate and said, "I don't care if every saint on earth dies of disease, the Word of God promises *me* healing and I take it, and I have it." I have had it ever since.

I may say that years after I met this lovely saint (I had not seen her for years and did not know if she was on earth or in the glory) in a great department store purchasing a new dress. That didn't look as though she contemplated casting off these earthly cerements. I took courage and approached her and a fresh surprise waited me. Her terrible illness had caused her to lose all her hair but now her beautiful, abundant silvery locks were a halo of glory around her face.

I stared at them until she said sweetly, "Were you looking at my hair, Lilian?"

"Is it real?" I stammered, forgetting my manners in my astonishment.

"Quite real. God gave it to me in answer to prayer. Do you like it?"

"Like is a feeble word; I love it, I never saw anything more heavenly in the way of hair."

The Bible says, "The hoary head is a crown of glory, if it be found in the way of righteousness," so perhaps I was not far wrong in calling her hair "heavenly." And while that dear woman was going on from faith to faith until she was able to pray the hair back on her head even in old age, I, at the enemy's behest, was beholding lying vanities and forsaking my own mercy until it nearly cost me my life.

A word to the wise is sufficient.

9

"Let Us Go Over unto the Other Side"

"Let us go over unto the other side" (Luke 8:22).
These words were addressed by the Lord Jesus
Christ to His disciples who were safely on board a
ship captained by the Creator of "all things visible
and invisible."

It was evening and Jesus was exceedingly weary
as the result of His labors with a multitude of people
who had just dispersed to their various homes. As He
lay asleep on a pillow in the rear of the boat, the
disciples obediently went about their various duties.

Possibly Peter's thoughts may have been something like this: "If the Master had not commanded it
— His very words were 'Let us go over unto the other
side' — I would never have ventured on the sea this
night. But no matter how the storm clouds lower, we
must be safe, for He is in the ship."

So they labored on in spite of rising wind, lash-
ing waves, and threatening skies. And "other little
ships" took courage to follow in the wake of the boat
which contained the Lord. But the tempest increased
in fury; the waves towered mountains high, beating

against the frail bark till its destruction seemed inevitable.

From their knowledge of seamanship the disciples were well aware that, barring a miracle, they were no better than dead men. Surely the Master will arise and come to their aid! Why this mysterious delay?

They venture to creep to His side and look upon the sublime spectacle of God incarnate, sleeping like a tired babe upon its mother's breast, while demons of hell shriek round the boat that cradles Omnipotence in a vain effort to founder it.

How profound is the peace that envelops the divine sleeper! Somehow they dare not disturb Him. His repose is so holy!

Meantime the ship is filling fast. Now it is full, and the sea is actually engulfing them. They are sinking into a watery grave.

As the pangs of death seize them, they cry in anguish, "Master, carest thou not that we perish? And he arose, and rebuked the wind, and said unto the sea, Peace, be still. And the wind ceased, and there was a great calm." The Lord can talk to the sea, rebuke the winds, speak to fish and birds — the fish released Jonah at His command, and the ravens obeyed Him.

If you have known what it is to have the tempest of sin, sickness, anxiety or sorrow stilled by that Voice, you know how great is the calm, how exquisite the relief, how unutterably glorious the deliverance that comes with His word of power.

With the disciples you cry, "What manner of man is this?" And you answer, "The God-Man, the Word made flesh, Immanuel, God with us."

This narrative is full of invaluable lessons to us.

Let us take heed how we hear! Note that, though He delivered them, the Lord was far from satisfied with the conduct of the disciples during the awful ordeal. He had a rebuke for them – and a scathing one – as well as for the elements warring under the command of the prince of the power of the air. For Satan had not only stirred up an awful storm on the Sea of Galilee but had succeeded in creating a tempest of unbelief in the hearts of the disciples.

The Lord Jesus told them that they were fearful for one reason alone, namely, because they had no faith. He had said, "Let us go *over*," and they should have known that they could not go *under*. Then again He said, "Let *us* go over," assuring them of His presence with them, so no evil could befall them.

Under similar circumstances Abraham would have known that he would land high and dry, safe and sound on the other side of the lake, even if the boat turned upside down. Of him it is said, "Under utterly hopeless circumstances he hopefully believed" (Romans 4:18, Weymouth).

Paul dared to stand forth when "all hope that we should be saved was then taken away" and say, "Be of good cheer: for there shall be no loss of any man's life among you" (Acts 27:20, 22). Why was he so fearless? He tells us in the 25th verse of the same chapter, "I believe God, that it shall be even as it was told me."

If a storm, whether of temptation, physical suffering and weakness, or financial disaster imperils your frail bark, ask yourself one question: "Is the Lord Jesus Christ on board?" Then follow it up with a second one if the answer to the first is in the affirmative, "Is He the Captain?" If you can answer these inquiries satisfactorily to your own conscience, enlightened by

the Word and the Holy Spirit, you are absolutely safe
from every ill. God will take care of you. I say it
most reverently, He *must* in order to be true to His
Word which He has magnified above His Name.

Let me relate a recent happening in my own im-
mediate environment. A young minister, a very con-
secrated man, an invaluable worker in the responsible
position he holds, was suddenly smitten with the most
direful symptoms, including excruciating abdominal
pains. He summoned God's servants, according to the
Scriptures, and earnest prayer was made for his relief.
The physical anguish subsided but later returned.

This was truly a tempest of satanic origin. As his
wife and children clustered about him and believers
stood fast holding on to God, an ambulance arrived,
and surgeons came to his bedside. They examined
him but said that they could not arrive at a diagnosis
without taking him to the sanitarium, and added that
as the case appeared to be a very serious one, there
should be no delay about doing this.

Truly the waves were dashing high, the lightnings
were flashing, and the thunders were rolling.

But, thank God, as he lifted his heart to heaven
for guidance he was reminded that he was called by
his Captain, the Lord Jesus, to "go over" from sickness
to health, by the prayer of faith (James 5:14), nothing
being said about "going under" an operation. So
commending himself to God he said, "I will trust and
not be afraid." And the word of power was spoken,
the wind ceased, and there was a great calm.

That was several months ago, and there has been
no return of the symptoms; and like the disciples after
they had crossed over at the Lord's command, he
has witnessed marvelous manifestations of God's healing power. His mother was healed of cancer (diagno-

sis made by one of the very best men in the large city
in which she lives), and his little girl was snatched
from the very jaws of death.

Another verified case came to my notice lately. A
woman was told that she must have her foot ampu-
tated. General septic poisoning was feared, I pre-
sume. She consulted the Lord and was given Proverbs
3:26, "For the Lord shall be thy confidence, and shall
keep thy foot from being taken." On that ship, with
the Lord in command, she safely weathered the storm
and came out on the other side high and dry, with
two perfectly good feet. Praise God for His faithfulness!

10

"Aeneas, Jesus Christ Cures You"

"Now Peter, as he went to town after town, came down also to God's people at Lydda. There he found a man by the name of Aeneas, who for eight years had kept his bed, through being paralyzed. Peter said to him, Aeneas, Jesus Christ cures you. Rise and make your own bed. He at once rose to his feet. And all the people of Lydda and Sharon saw him; and they turned to the Lord" (Acts 9:32-35, Weymouth).

Here is a case of healing of hopeless chronic disease which took place after Christ's ascension, in the present dispensation of the Holy Spirit.

If the eye of some sufferer from chronic disease is scanning this page, let me lovingly entreat him to pray, before reading further, in the words of the psalmist, "Open thou mine eyes, that I may behold wondrous things out of thy law. . . . Make me to understand the way of thy precepts: so shall I talk of thy wondrous works" (Psalm 119:18, 27). For in these brief verses *opened* eyes behold the truth, "and the truth shall make you free."

To such, "talking of His wondrous works" becomes

the one purpose in life, and there is no power on earth or in hell that can shut their mouths once their eyes have been opened to see the risen Christ as their life, physical as well as spiritual.

Can you not see in this Scripture passage busy Peter hurrying from town to town, ministering everywhere in the "power of His resurrection," reaching Lydda and being lovingly greeted by the brethren there?

It is probably not long before some brother says to the apostle, "We have a very sad case here. A man by the name of Aeneas who has been bedfast for eight long years. Could you visit him? He is a great sufferer."

And as the apostle stands by that bed of pain, Aeneas' sad eyes that have looked so long for deliverance in vain are fixed upon his face. What does Peter do? Nothing. He knows better than to try to do anything but fade out of the picture and let the One who has already done it all shine forth in all His power and glory — the One by whose stripes Aenaes was healed already if he would only believe it.

"Aeneas, *Jesus Christ* cures you." The messenger delivers his message; the "interpreter, one among a thousand" brings the sufferer face to face with Jesus, anointed with the Holy Spirit and with power "who went about doing good and healing all."

One look of faith to the risen One and Aeneas' eyes, sad no longer, flash with superabundant vitality. He rises immediately. We can't blame him for being in something of a hurry to get up after eight years of helpless recumbency.

He makes his own bed, as Peter told him to do. What a luxury after being hauled and mauled round by well-meaning but oftentimes awkward people who ministered to his helplessness! Only those who know by sad experience what it means to lie an inert mass of flesh at the mercy of others, can appreciate Aeneas' feelings on this joyful occasion. How he enjoyed walking! And by merely walking about and letting people see him do it, he is used to bring about a revival that sweeps all the people of Lydda and Sharon into the fountain of cleansing. "All that dwelt at Lydda and Sharon saw him, and turned to the Lord" (Acts 9:35). Worthwhile, wasn't it?

As I meditate over this account, a question continually rises in my mind: If the Word of God says of Aeneas, "Jesus maketh thee *whole*," have we any right to be one half or even three quarters whole? If Peter told Aeneas, "Jesus Christ cures you," are we justified in remaining sick? Or was this wonderful gift only for Aeneas and some other special favorites?

I think we can find the answer to this query in Luke 4:16-30. Jesus had returned to His home town after going about all Galilee, teaching, preaching, and healing. His fame had gone forth and He well knew that His fellow townsmen felt that they had a special claim upon Him. "Ye will surely say . . . Physician, heal thyself: whatsoever we have heard done in Capernaum, do also here in thy country."

Knowing their attitude He reads, when the roll is given Him, from Isaiah 61, where it is written, "The Spirit of the Lord is upon me, because he hath anointed me to preach the gospel to the poor; he hath sent me to heal the broken hearted, to preach deliverance to the captives, and recovering of sight to the blind, to set at liberty them that are bruised, to preach the acceptable year of the Lord."

Then closing the book and sitting down, when all eyes are fastened upon Him, He said unto them, "This

day is this scripture fulfilled in your ears." In other
words He proclaimed salvation, healing, deliverance,
the opening of blind eyes, physical and spiritual, for
all who would accept it, then and there. Nobody in
Nazareth need to let the sun set that night upon their
sin, sickness, affliction, or captivity. What a jubilee
they might have celebrated! What a revival would
inevitably have resulted!

What hindered? One thing only — their failure to
acknowledge, accept, believe upon, and submit to the
Word of God made flesh, who stood among them
offering Himself freely to all. "He sent His Word and
healed them." But what if they will not take the
medicine? "I would, . . . but ye would not." Naaman
humbled himself, believed the message in the mouth of
a serving maid, obeyed God and was healed. The
widow of Sarepta believed so thoroughly that she took
the bread from the mouth of her son who was threatened with death from famine, at God's command, and
both she and her son, and her house, were saved
from death. If you really believe the promise, you will
obey the precept that accompanies it.

"Aeneas, Jesus Christ cures you." Put your name,
whether James, John, Jacob, Joy, or whatever it may
be, in place of Aeneas in this verse and *believe* it.
Your disease will vanish — I say it on the authority
of the Word of God — "I am the Lord that healeth
thee"; "I am the Lord, I change not." It matters not
whether your ailment is acute or chronic, "He healeth
all thy diseases." And when you step forth, you will
find that your "Lydda and Sharon" will turn to the
Lord.

God Called Abraham Alone

Among the most vivid recollections of my early childhood is the story of my mother's wedding dress. I never saw the garment, as it was unfortunately stolen before I was born. Perhaps that made it all the more interesting. At any rate I shall never forget the description of its beauty and costliness which always ended with, "It was real silk brocade, from London, and would *stand alone.*" (The last two words always very emphatic.)

I never quite understood what "standing alone" as applied to a dress meant, nor why it was deemed an essential quality for a perfect wedding gown, but I listened with almost reverential awe nevertheless.

There is another wedding dress I want us to consider, the wedding garment of the bride of the Lamb. This dress is of "fine linen, clean and white; for the fine linen is the righteousness of saints (Revelation 19:7, 8). In other words, it is "the righteousness of God which is by faith of Jesus Christ unto all and upon all them that believe" (Romans 3:22). Here is a wedding dress that will "stand alone."

Real faith will stand alone anywhere for any length

of time in the face of all contradictions and in the
teeth of any opposition, for it rests on the "forever
settled" Word of God.

> There's a walk for every soul in God alone,
>   There's a stand in God for every soul to take.
> There's a walk none else can take but only you,
>   For this path is trod by you and God alone.
> He calls, He apprehends your soul to stand in Him,
> And as you praise and stand the work is done.
>   God called Abraham alone!

Yes, God called Abraham alone and blessed him
and increased him (Isaiah 51:2).

As I read the story of the healing of Blind Bartimaeus, the Holy Spirit impressed me of this man's
aloneness with God throughout the entire transaction
(Mark 10:46-52). There he sat, alone in a crowd —
the loneliest kind of loneliness — hopeless and helpless. No one volunteered a hand to assist him to get
within range of the Great Physician.

But he could *hear* and he used what he *had* to se-
cure what he *lacked*. The moment his ears told him
that it was Jesus of *Nazareth* who was passing by
(many were called Jesus in that day), he filled his
lungs and emitted a cry so piercing that it brought
down stern rebukes on his head. For Jesus of *Nazareth* was He who said, "The Spirit of the Lord is upon
me, because he hath anointed me to preach the
gospel to the poor; he hath sent me to heal the broken-
hearted, to preach deliverance to the captives, and
recovering of sight to the blind, to set at liberty them
that are bruised, to preach the acceptable year of the
Lord" (Luke 4:18, 19).

Poor blind beggar! How easily the crowd could
have silenced him forcibly. But Bartimaeus had lost

all consciousness of the crowd. By faith he wrenched himself clean out of his surroundings and stood alone with God incarnate in the person of His Son, Jesus Christ the Lord. There were to him just two people present, Jesus of Nazareth, and the blind beggar, Bartimaeus.

Alone and unaided by any favoring circumstance, he undertook by his voice, the only thing he had, to bring the two into vital contact. Opposition only made him cry the "more a great deal." That is its invariable effect on real faith, for real faith will stand alone. "And Jesus stood still!" Amazing words! His every step controlled and directed by the Spirit of God, Jesus was on an errand to some definite objective, yet at the cry of Bartimaeus — no, at the cry of *faith* — He stood still.

Marvel of marvels, God incarnate, Creator and Sustainer of the universe, arrested in His course, brought to a full stop by a blind beggar's cry. Yes, for "all things are possible to him that believeth."

Bartimaeus received his sight and followed Jesus in the way.

12

"Our Daily Bread"

"And he said unto them, When ye pray, say, Our
Father which art in heaven, . . . give us day by day
our daily bread" (Luke 11:2, 3).

The Lord Jesus Christ asked His Father, with
utter simplicity and child-like confidence, for His
bread, a day's supply at a time.

The Father of our Lord Jesus Christ is our Father,
too, by virtue of the new birth; and we should ask Him
for our bread just as confidently as our elder Brother
did, realizing that our Father heareth us always, and
we have only to ask in order to receive. What prob-
lems would be solved, what anxieties stilled, what cares
banished if we always did this!

> If our love were but more simple
> We should take Him at His Word
> And our lives would be all sunshine
> In the sweetness of our Lord.

The Lord Jesus knew, as we never can know, what
intricate adjustments and complex arrangements have
to be effected by divine wisdom and omnipotence in

order to answer that simple little petition that any tiny child can breathe, "Give us our daily bread."

When have we our daily bread? When we have a bank account, or a meal ticket reposes safely in our pocket, or we have a standing invitation to the hospitable board of some kind friend? No indeed; in any and all of these situations we may still be far from our daily bread.

Driving through thousands of acres of golden grain in the Canadian Northwest, I said to myself, "There's our daily bread from our Father's hand." Then, as I watched the men working like tigers to gather the precious grain before the frost or storm could blight it, I said, "And our Father knows that it is good for us to eat our bread in the sweat of our faces, and so He lets us work hard for it and do much toward answering our own prayers."

But as in thought I turned from the external and apparent to the internal and invisible and remembered the elaborate process and complex changes every atom of food has to undergo before it can be utilized by the system, I changed my tune and said, "Oh, the work those men are doing is just child's play; they are . . . like little ones running errands for Mother who is doing all the real work. God alone can give us our daily bread."

When have we our daily bread? When we take it into our mouths, taste, masticate, and swallow it? By no means. Do you realize that you are inconceivably complex, made up of millions of units, microscopic cells, each of which is eagerly waiting for its daily bread, and a goodly number of which require a special diet to enable them to perform peculiar functions upon which the continuance of life depends?

When you say, "Give us this day our daily bread,"

you are praying for the necessary food supplies for a whole community, so to speak. And the raw materials which you take into your mouth have to be acted upon by a number of secretions of various organs, beginning with the salivary glands in the mouth, passing on to the gastric juice of the stomach, pancreatic juice from the pancreas, and so on through the intestines, being modified during the whole progress by glandular secretions of the most complex chemical nature poured in from the various organs.

Not until this work is fully accomplished and the digested food is carried into the circulation and duly distributed do the cells hear the dinner bell and get their daily bread. So essential is every detail to the answer to the prayer, "Give us our daily bread," that failure at one point may be fatal even to life itself.

For example, sugar is necessary to life, and normal blood contains it in the proportion of 1-1000. But before the sugar taken with the food can be utilized by the body cells, which cannot exist without it, it has to be acted upon by a glandular secretion produced in the so-called "islets" of the pancreas, from which fact it takes its name "insulin" (Latin *insula,* an island).

In the absence of insulin the sugar taken into the system is thrown into the blood as refuse, and upon the kidneys devolves the task of excreting it. Meantime the cells are starving for sugar, and ultimately the individual dies of sugar starvation with his blood loaded with it — just as a man may die for lack of water in an open boat in the middle of the ocean.

Surely we are "fearfully and wonderfully made!" Well might the Lord Jesus say, "Take no thought . . . what ye shall eat, or what ye shall drink. . . . Is not the *life* more than meat?" (Matthew 6:25).

What is the corollary from all this? God and God alone can give us our daily bread. We may have it in the bank, in our hands, in our mouths, in our stomachs, in our blood even, but only God can *give* it to us. This He does by making His Word health to all our flesh, including every gland and cell.

So this beautiful prayer, "Give us this day our daily bread," is a petition not for food only but for *life*, which is more than meat. In other words it is a prayer for *perfect health* put in our mouths by the Lord Jesus Himself.

13

A Miracle That Speaks to Our Own Times

"Jesus came again into Cana of Galilee, where he made the water wine. And there was a certain nobleman, whose son was sick at Capernaum. When he heard that Jesus was come out of Judea into Galilee, he went unto him, and besought him that he would come down, and heal his son: for he was at the point of death. Then said Jesus unto him, Except ye see signs and wonders, ye will not believe. The nobleman saith unto him, Sir, come down ere my child die. Jesus saith unto him, Go thy way; thy son liveth. And the man believed the word that Jesus had spoken unto him, and he went his way. And as he was now going down, his servants met him, and told him, saying, Thy son liveth. Then enquired he of them the hour when he began to amend. And they said unto him, Yesterday at the seventh hour the fever left him. So the father knew that it was at the same hour in which Jesus said unto him, Thy son liveth; and himself believed, and his whole house" (John 4:46-53).

The Bible states that Jesus came into Cana of Galilee, where He had made the water wine. Close at hand was Capernaum, where dwelt many Roman officials in their beautiful mansions. From the Greek it is evident that the man of this story was a ruler, or courtier, a resident of Capernaum.

It is possible, probable, perhaps almost certain, that he had heard of the first miracle, for we read in John 2:11, "This beginning of miracles did Jesus in Cana of Galilee, and *manifested forth his glory; and his disciples believed on him.*" It is within the bounds of possibility that he was present at the wedding ceremony. He may have been an eye-witness of the marvel and tasted of the water that was made wine. From the perturbation manifested when the supply of wine proved insufficient, the family may well have been prominent persons in the society of the district. What better lesson in faith could he have had than the miracle at the wedding? God expected him to profit by it, and He expects us to profit by similar experiences.

There was a need, a real need, a great one. No wine? Forever and forever in the conservative East this would be quoted against the honor of the family, "The wine gave out at the wedding!" The mother of the Lord Jesus revealed to Him the awful situation. "They have no wine!" And then, confident that He would do something though His words sounded discouraging, she said to the servants. "Whatsoever he saith unto you, do it." He will speak, only believe and obey, no matter what He tells you to do.

That is *faith.* "*Whatsoever he saith unto you, do it.*" If He tells you to walk when you have no legs, step out; or to speak when you have no voice, open your mouth wide immediately; or to believe when you are not conscious of an atom of faith, do it; or to sing His praises when you feel like chanting a dirge, shout, "I will extol Thee, my God. . . . I will bless thy name forever and ever." That is *faith*.

When He spoke, He told them to fill up the water-pots. A hard task; their combined capacity was about 162 gallons. "*Whatsoever*." No doubt the water had to be carried some distance, and what use would it be when they brought it? It was wine, not water, that was needed. "*Whatsoever*." And they filled them to the brim.

Then came a much harder test. (They always get harder as you go from faith to greater faith.)

"Draw out now, and bear unto the governor of the feast."

"But it is *water!*"

"*Whatsoever!*" And they obeyed. And when the governor had tasted it — I don't believe there was any change till then — he said, "Well, this is good wine for sure!"

This Roman nobleman who approached Jesus concerning his son presumably had this happening to go upon, and he asked the Lord Jesus to "come down" and heal his son, lying at the point of death. He wanted the personal, physical, visible presence of the Lord. That's what we want and what we lack. So this miracle is specially suited to our own time and condition.

Once my sister and I were having a great test of faith. We had the promise, but our eyes failed to report anything, our ears gave no testimony to its fulfillment, though the Word said, "It is finished." We wanted the Lord Jesus to "come down" and show us "signs and wonders." But that was not to be. Instead the Holy Spirit sang a song through my sister, one verse of which was:

> Let Me *close* the eyes of your *senses*
>   And *open* your *heavenly sight;*
> For only thus shalt thou see Me
>   In that world of which I am the Light;
> And thus thou mayest now behold Me,
>   Fully trust My power divine,
> And sing the song of the ages long,
>   "I am Thine, and Thou art mine."

Let us note three points:

1. Distance was no obstacle to the Lord Jesus then, and it is no obstacle to Him now. He healed this child by His word, in spite of intervening distance. He will do the same for you or me if we trust Him. In view of the fact that man has largely annihilated distance by his inventions, such as rapid transportation, radio, telephone, wireless, telegraph, television, etc., and executives of great corporations daily contact London, New York, Tokyo, Bombay, Melbourne, or any other part of the earth, and make their power felt wherever they desire, surely it is not hard to believe that distance is no barrier to the working of the divine will in the fulfillment of His Word.

2. This miracle of healing was performed in answer to simple faith in the word of God. The Lord Jesus Christ led the seeker away from everything but His word. "Except you see signs and wonders you will not believe" (John 4:48). Then He tested him with a word. The word of the Lord *tries* you. It tried Joseph when he was in prison (Psalm 105:19). Never say that you "tried divine healing." The Word of God is tried "as silver tried in a furnace of earth, purified seven times" (Psalm 12:6). Divine healing,

which is the Word of God, tries you and me. God grant we may not be found wanting!

The Lord Jesus gave the father the word, "Go thy way; thy son liveth" (John 4:50). The man met the test, and believed the naked word. He ceased all clamor for the Lord to come to his home and went quietly about his business.

3. This case was definitely gradual in its manifestation. The healing "began" at a certain moment. Temperature went down to normal at the "seventh hour" (John 4:52). The boy became convalescent. In other words, it was not a case of instantaneous healing, like most of those in the ministry of the Lord. In the 8th chapter of Matthew, for instance, we have three cases of instantaneous healing in the first fifteen verses: the leper who was cleansed "immediately," the centurion's servant "healed in the self same hour," and Peter's mother-in-law, who rose and ministered to them when Jesus touched her. On the other hand, we see many gradual healings in our own day; though praise God! dazzling miracles are still seen, sometimes lightning-like in their manifestation.

Is there such a thing as having *gradual* faith? Is it possible that the father in this true story possessed it? Notice that he asked when his son *"began to amend."* We might modernize that into "When did he show the first symptoms of improvement?"

Let us never forget that the unchanging law is "As thou hast believed, so be it done unto thee" (Matthew 8:13).

14

"A Spirit of Infirmity"

"And he was teaching in one of the synagogues on the sabbath. And, behold, there was a woman which had a spirit of infirmity eighteen years, and was bowed together, and could in no wise lift up herself. And when Jesus saw her, he called her to him, and said unto her, Woman, thou art loosed from thine infirmity. And he laid his hands on her; and immediately she was made straight, and glorified God. And the ruler of the synagogue answered with indignation, because that Jesus had healed on the sabbath day, and said unto the people, There are six days in which men ought to work, in them therefore come and be healed, and not on the sabbath day. The Lord then answered him, and said, Thou hypocrite, doth not each one of you on the sabbath loose his ox or his ass from the stall, and lead him away to watering? And ought not this woman, being a daughter of Abraham, whom Satan hath bound, lo, these eighteen years, be loosed from this bond on the sabbath day? And when he had said these things, all his adversaries were ashamed; and all the people rejoiced for all the glorious things that were done by him."

Time — the Sabbath day, a sacred time.

Place — a synagogue, a sacred place.

Act — Healing, a sacred thing, part of redemption (Isaiah 53:4).

Case — paralysis, accompanied by hideous, repulsive deformity (Luke 13:11).

Character — Chronic, of eighteen years' standing. Hopeless.

Call — The Lord Jesus Christ summoned the sufferer to Him. We beg and plead and pray while all the time Jesus is calling us to leave all else and come to Him. He sees us in our sickness. He saw that sufferer because He was looking for that sort of thing. He said, "The whole need not a physician; but they that are sick" (Luke 5:31). If you are sick, He is calling you — "Come unto me, all ye that . . . are heavy laden" (Matthew 11:28).

Cause — As given by the Great Physician, Satan (Luke 13:16). What a flood of illumination is here thrown on many cases of suffering! Jesus did not ascribe this case to natural causes. He distinctly declared that it had a supernatural origin and was inflicted by Satan himself, through the agency of an evil spirit. A "spirit of infirmity" saps the power out of muscle, nerve, and tendon so that they cannot support the body in its normal posture. I have seen cases of this character, and, thank God, I have witnessed their deliverance through the power of the Name of the Lord Jesus Christ. Note that our Lord does not recognize this disease as a providential dispensation but speaks of it as the direct result of Satan's devices.

Fault-finders — Certainly. They are always present when God is working. Satan takes care of that. Jesus answered them and made them ashamed (vv. 14-16). He will answer them for you, too, by mighty mani-

festations of His power if you contend earnestly for
the faith once delivered to the saints. The signs will
follow the Word faithfully preached (Mark 16:20).
Fault-finders will be confounded by your lips *and life*.

Condition of Healing — Faith (v. 16). A faith
like Abraham's believes without seeing in the face of
seeming impossibilities and acts on God's Word alone.
Noah began building an ark on dry ground by faith
in God's word which proclaimed the coming of the
Deluge. Dr. Simpson began to build a life work for
God on an existence which physicians pronounced at
an end. No, it was on God's Word which said, "I am
the Lord that healeth thee" (Exodus 15:26).

Cable — Binding God and Man. "Ought." The
most powerful word in human language for it implies
moral obligation. God says that the sick *ought* to be
healed, and He was so determined to heal them that
He allowed His Son to bear such awful atrocities that
His mangled body lost almost the semblance of humanity (Isaiah 52:14). By His shed blood He made
provision for the cleansing of all sin from every human soul, and by His broken body He provided perfect soundness for every human body born into this
world. God acknowledges the force of this "ought"
and has fully met His responsibility. Now it remains
for us to discharge ours by entering into our heritage
by faith.

15

Jesus in His Home Town

"And he came to Nazareth, where he had been brought up: and, as his custom was, he went into the synagogue on the sabbath day and stood up for to read. And there was delivered unto him the book of the prophet Esaias. And when he had opened the book, he found the place where it was written, The Spirit of the Lord is upon me, because he hath anointed me to preach the gospel to the poor; he hath sent me to heal the broken-hearted, to preach deliverance to the captives, and recovering of sight to the blind, to set at liberty them that are bruised. To preach the acceptable year of the Lord ["to proclaim the year of acceptance with the Lord" — Weymouth]. And he closed the book, and he gave it again to the minister, and sat down. And the eyes of all them that were in the synagogue were fastened on him. And he began to say unto them, This day is this scripture fulfilled in your ears" ["in your hearing" — Weymouth] (Luke 4:16-21).

This is a most striking incident which reminds me of one that occurred in my own ministry. I was holding meetings, which were being very well attended, in a prosperous rural district. On one occasion I was clearly guided to ask a young farmer, son of a very godly family, to give the message at an evening meeting. He did not want to say yes, dreading to face his old friends in the capacity of a preacher, and he dared not say no, for he was not sure that God did not demand it of him. So he went away and waited on the Lord with the result that it was revealed to him that he was to preach that evening, and tell his friends and neighbors that the call of God was upon him to devote every moment to the service of the Lord in the ministry. Never shall I forget his simplicity and humility.

He said, "I was asked to preach this evening; and when I asked the Lord if He wanted me to do it, He said to me, 'I don't want you to do anything else as long as you live.' Well, boys, whatever you think of my preaching, I am sure there's one thing you will never say and that is that I went to preaching because I didn't love farming." I think it possible that there wasn't a dry eye in the church when his message was finished.

And the inhabitants of Nazareth were touched by the presence of the gentle Nazarene who had grown up in their midst. No doubt He had done little carpenter jobs for them when He was helping Joseph. Some of the mothers in Israel had handed Him some little "goodies" when He was still a child and had seen the heavenly light in His eyes as He lifted His eyes and thanked them.

Then, too, there hung about Him the halo of notoriety, for "there went out a fame of Him through all the region round about. And He taught in their synagogues, being glorified of all" (Luke 4:14, 15). No wonder that the eyes of all were fastened upon

Him as He began to speak. And what a message it
was — no, *is!* For He is the same today and says the
same word of power. He cannot change. He proclaimed unto them the fulfillment of the words of the
prophet, uttered seven hundred years before. He
proclaims to us their fulfillment today, for He says, "I
am the Lord, I change not" (Malachi 3:6).

Then He answered their thoughts, for they were
saying in their hearts, "If all these wonders we hear
He has performed elsewhere really took place, let us
see some of the same sort here. There is plenty of
sickness and suffering, poverty, and blindness in Nazareth. Physician, heal thyself. Minister to your own
townsmen who have the first claim upon you."

And He did not withdraw His gracious offer, did
not modify His claims in the smallest degree. He said
in effect "the only hindrance to My doing the same
works I have performed elsewhere lies in you. You do
not accept Me for what I am. 'No prophet is accepted in his own country.' God is the same, He is
unchanging. He is the same to you that He was to
Naaman. But your attitude toward God is not that of
Naaman. He received God's messenger and obeyed
his command. He humbled himself to the very dust
before God as He was represented in the message
of His messenger. When the prophet did not come
out and speak to him, he did as he was commanded
and dove seven times into Jordan. Thus Naaman received healing, and so will anyone else who will follow
his example. It cannot be otherwise, for God is the
same God to you that He was to Naaman."

And the audience immediately proved the truth of
His words concerning them. For they were so proud,
not humble like Naaman, that His words turned their
kindness toward Him to absolute hatred, and they

tried to murder Him then and there by casting Him headlong over the hill on which Nazareth was built.

They desired to be healed no doubt. They could have been healed had they met the conditions, for God is unchanging. They could not be healed without meeting the conditions, for God is unchanging.

Now if you desire to be healed and are not healed, there has to be a change. And that change must be in you, for God never changes. He is the Lord that healeth "all thy diseases." If you will humble yourself before Him and pray believingly, He will reveal to you exactly what the needed change is. More than that, He will enable you to make it. "For it is God which worketh in you both to will and to do of His good pleasure" (Phil. 2:13).

16

The Voice of Elijah

"And the Lord heard the voice of Elijah; and the soul of the child came into him again, and he revived" (1 Kings 17:22).

This is a lesson on the power of prayer, spoken prayer, in the ministry of divine healing.

You remember the story; Elijah, that mighty man of God, had come by divine command from his refuge at Cherith to Zarephath to be sustained by a widow.

What a test it was for his faith to be obliged to leave Cherith! The word means "promise," and God had said, "Hide thyself by the brook Cherith, that is before Jordan. And it shall be that thou shalt drink of the brook; and I have commanded the ravens to feed thee *there*" (1 Kings 17:3, 4).

And as he sat by the brook that flowed through the rocky gorge, it seemed to sing as it rippled, "*God* is faithful, God is faithful. He will always keep His Word, to the uttermost fulfilling every promise I have heard." How sweet, so pure and sparkling the waters were to his lips!

And the punctuality of the ravens, never failing to

bring bread and flesh in the morning and bread and flesh in the evening, solemn and stately in their black plumage as so many servitors in some palace!

"And he drank of the brook." Oh, Cherith is a delightful place in which to dwell! Never shall I forget a sojourn there! The Lord told us to name our home Cherith and put it on an electric light on the front door. He gave my sister a song which began —

> Oh, the earth was very dry,
> Parched beneath a brazen sky;
> Humbly see the prophet stand,
> Listening to his God's command —
> "Go to Cherith, I will feed thee there;
> Go to Cherith, drink its waters fair.
> Lo, I speak to fish and bird,
> My commands the ravens heard,
> Go to Cherith, I will feed thee there."

But the brook dried up! Explain that if you can; I can't, and I know better than to try. What is to be done in a case like that? What did Elijah do? Listened for the next command. "Whatsoever He saith unto you do it." That is all we need.

"And the word of the Lord *came*" (1 Kings 17: 8). It always does when we listen for it with a fixed determination to obey. "Arise." Take higher ground. "Get thee to Zarephath. . . . I have commanded a widow woman there to sustain thee."

Zarephath means fiery furnace, crucible. Yes, the gold must be further refined, for there is stern work to be done, and Zarephath is the place for the refining process.

When Elijah arrived at Zarephath, the widow was on the spot as promptly as were the ravens. But what

a change in the menu! And what unutterable humilia-
tion for the prophet to order a cake made from meal
snatched from the mouth of a child ready to die of
starvation and watered with the mother's tears! And
yet what glorious things God was bestowing on that
widow! He is the husband of the widow and the
father of the fatherless.

I remember a widow of my acquaintance and a
little incident in her life that may seem an inter-
polation, but I believe it belongs here. She was living
by faith, and that encouraged her to take in boys
and young men who were not always able to pay their
board promptly. She felt she could trust God for
them and help them spiritually. God never failed her,
but one Saturday she had a hard test. She had prepared a big baking, bread, buns, pies, and cakes for
Sunday, so as to be able to be free for worship on the
Lord's day. Going to the coal bin she found, to her
dismay, that she could not possibly bake the things
she had made because of the shortage of coal. Some
of the boys who were at home followed her footsteps
and laughed loudly when they realized her predica-
ment.

"Now, Mother, what are you going to do? Look at
that bread rising fast; and your coal has given out."

"Well, God hasn't given out," she answered. "I
am going to have a little talk with Jesus." And she
vanished to the attic which was her sanctuary. But
before she could get on her knees there was a loud
call from the boys downstairs:

"Mother, come down. Here is a load of coal."

Sure enough there was a man at the door with a
truck load of coal.

"I didn't order any coal."

"Well, it is for this number" the man replied.

"Take it away. I never order coal unless I have money on hand to pay for it. There's some mistake."

And she retraced her steps to the attic, leaving the boys, who were much interested in the baking of the pies, disappointed. Closing her eyes she began to pray; but before she could frame a petition, the Lord said, "Open your eyes, the answer is before you." And she opened her eyes and saw something she had been unconscious of before: rows and rows of old, worn-out boots and shoes. They had been given her for her boys. Instantly she understood and filled her apron with them and sent the boys up for more, till everything was baked. Just as the last pie was coming out, the truck returned with the coal and a message that it was paid for by a friend.

The widow of Zarephath stood the test. She literally took the last morsel from her son to feed the prophet. That was real faith. Of course there was no famine in that home after that. There could not be. But there was a crucible for her as well as for Elijah. The presence of the man of God brought awful conviction to her heart. We are not told what her concealed sin was, but she herself acknowledged that it merited no less punishment than the death of her son. As the child lay there dying, she confessed and found mercy (Proverbs 28:13).

If you have on your conscience unconfessed sin, my advice to you is to go at once to God and pour out your heart to Him. It is no use to seek for physical healing unless you are prepared to do this.

"Doesn't God ever heal unsaved people?" That is not the question. It is not for us to set limits to the grace of God. But as sin is the first cause of sickness, we cannot expect to be delivered from the latter while we are hugging to our bosoms the serpent who produces the deadly virus. When I struck an epidemic of typhoid my first step was to shut off the source of the disease.

Elijah, as the servant of God, now takes the case into his own hands. He says, "Give me thy son" (1 Kings 17:19). That means leave the case in God's hands. Take your hands and *eyes off.* How the distracted mother would cling to the little form, watching for some sign of returning animation! It might not be. Watching to see if God is healing is unbelief, pure and simple. "And he took him out of her bosom." And she let him do it! If you have never had an experience like that, you will not understand the depth of meaning covered by the simple words. Perhaps you will recall them and understand them better some day.

Elijah took the lad up to the loft, where he abode, and laid him upon his own bed. And he cried unto the Lord. *"And the Lord heard the voice of Elijah."* Oh, the power of the human voice! It can speak life or death. The judge says, "I sentence you to die," and the prisoner at the bar is legally dead from the moment the words are uttered. The power of the human voice, *speaking to God in believing prayer, is limitless.*

God heard the voice of Elijah and the child revived! Do you desire something from God? Let Him hear your voice, in confession of sin if necessary, like the widow of Zarephath, and in believing prayer, like Elijah, and *God will answer you.*